The Story of
MATTHEW DEREMER

FINDING LEVEL GROUND

SHIRLEY JUMP

Copyright © 2017 by NOW SC Press

All rights reserved. No part of this publication may be reproduced, distributed, or transmitted in any form or by any means, including photocopying, recording, or other electronic or mechanical methods, without the prior written permission of the publisher, except in the case of brief quotations embodied in critical reviews and certain other noncommercial uses permitted by copyright law. For permission requests, write to the publisher, addressed "Attention: Permissions Coordinator," via the website below.

1.888.5069-NOW
www.nowscpress.com
@nowscpress

Ordering Information:

Quantity sales. Special discounts are available on quantity purchases by corporations, associations, and others. For details, contact the publisher at the address above.

Orders by U.S. trade bookstores and wholesalers. Please contact: NOW SC Press: Tel: (888) 5069-NOW or visit www.nowscpress.com.

Printed in the United States of America

First Printing, 2017

ISBN: 978-0-9995845-6-9 Finding Level Ground

Bible Translations are from New International Version®

Table of Contents

Foreword 1

Introduction 5

Chapter One 9

Chapter Two 19

Chapter Three 27

Chapter Four 35

Chapter Five 41

Chapter Six 47

Chapter Seven 53

Chapter Eight 59

Chapter Nine 67

Chapter Ten 71

Chapter Eleven 75

Chapter Twelve 81

Chapter Thirteen 87

Chapter Fourteen 93

A Word from the Family 97

Afterword and Resources 103

Resources 107

FOREWORD

Matthew DeRemer caught me by surprise.

He blew into our church building one day full of anxiety, frustration, and fear. Talking to him, I discovered why this young man sought me out. He candidly revealed he was looking for answers to questions in his life that didn't make much sense to him; he was trying to reconcile his suffering and find level ground.

Through decades of meeting with people in counseling situations, I'm bombarded most often by this question: What do I do when it doesn't make sense?

I asked that question a few weeks ago during a message I was presenting at BridgePoint Church—the same BridgePoint you will read about in the following pages. When I decided to talk about it publicly and began to craft my message, I knew there wasn't a simple answer. Life is often difficult. It comes with a myriad of unanticipated situations and unexpected challenges. Some are extremely complicated—but does the answer to that question have to be? Complicated, I mean.

What if the answer to our most complicated, tragic, and difficult experiences is really simple? It doesn't make the journey any less difficult. It doesn't mean the process is any less arduous. Often, though, we find the simplest response is the most comforting and sufficient.

Matthew's story is difficult and complicated. He recognized this while he was still alive, and we who have survived him know it even more now. At first, even second glance, it doesn't make sense. There doesn't seem to be any feasible explanation for why a bright and vibrant life, gaining momentum and stability, would be taken in such a tragic way. Why, in the prime of his life, with so much more to give, would a life like Matthew's be snuffed out so senselessly?

In our grief and reckoning, we are haunted by these lingering questions. So, what do we do?

I have to be honest, in times when my faith in God is tested, my trust muscles are awfully weak. I want desperately to have confidence and hope for the future—but, if I'm being real, trust is challenging for me. However difficult, I've learned that one thing is true: trust is the best answer.

One of my favorite verses is Proverbs 3:5-6, "*Trust in the Lord with all your heart, and do not lean on your own understanding. In all your ways acknowledge him, and he will make straight your paths.*"

I don't know about you, but my problem is that I often lean toward my "own understanding" and away from God. Instead, I have to fight daily to lean towards the one who can carry me through every season of my life, regardless of whether it makes sense to me. That's trust. That's faith.

I've wrestled with God and pushed back about this topic more than any other, but I've come to discover that trust is really not that complicated. It's a choice. You and I get a choice each and every day to choose faith.

That day in my office, with Matthew sitting across from me, I shared that idea. His problem was the same as mine—he kept trying to lean on his own understanding. He was trying to figure it all out for himself, get his most burning questions answered and packed neatly away. He lacked faith.

I told Matthew that he looked like a guy who was running down a hill covered with gravel. To everyone around, he looked like a strong, healthy guy out for a run down a hill. He was the only one that knew that he was one step from face-planting into the rocks. He looked like he was in control, but in reality, the hill and the gravel had taken over. He was on his feet but was completely out of control. He looked up at me with tears in his eyes and said, "That's it! That's me! I am NOT in control!"

Next, I told him that what I was about to say wouldn't make sense, but it was exactly what he needed to do: lean in and fully lose control.

"As long as you are trying to control your own life, you're going to be frustrated and anxious—but the moment you let go of that control and let God have your life, you'll find the peace you so desperately desire."

He thought about what I offered him and finally countered, "It's risky."

I agreed, it was a risk. "But what do you have that you're so scared to lose? Control? Fear? Anxiety? Isn't that worth the risk?"

"Can it really be that simple?" He responded.

I told him, "Yes!"

As you read his story, I hope that you also discover the simplicity of trust. I hope you find faith, the same faith Matthew found in my office. The same faith his family found. A powerful, relentless faith that carries us through the inevitable periods of life that don't make sense.

Pastor Tim Whipple
BridgePoint Church

Introduction

I met Matt DeRemer in the summer of 2015. I was facilitating a marriage development learning group at BridgePoint Church on Tuesday evenings. Earlier that afternoon, I received a call from one of the pastors at church telling me that we would have a new young man joining our class that evening. Another gentleman served as the co-facilitator of the group and I decided to pass the new arrival over to him because he was much more experienced than I with this kind of thing. At the last minute, my partner had a conflict and couldn't make it that night.

Matt showed up at the beginning of class dressed in his biker leathers. He seemed a bit intimidating, but was polite and respectful. He sat quietly and listened intently to the group discussion, but I could tell something was bothering him. As the class ended, Matt came up to me and asked if we could talk.

I said, "Sure, what's up?" and in the next few minutes, Matt's story exploded out of him. He told me that his wife had left him. She wouldn't speak to him and he wanted to get her back so they could make the marriage work. They had only been married three weeks. He told me they were believers and asked me again what he needed to do to get his wife back.

I'll never forget the look on his face when I told him that he needed to let his wife go and let God deal with her right now, while Matt focused on his relationship with Jesus Christ. He was angry—perhaps he wanted a quicker fix than the answer I gave him. We spoke a little more, but Matt was still upset and agitated. I told Matt I would be praying for both him and his wife, then I handed him my business card and told him he could call me 24/7.

I really thought that was the last time I would see Matt. God had other plans, though, and Matt called me about a week later. We ended up talking every few days for several months. Our conversations centered on letting God be God and falling in love with Jesus Christ. I gave him a few books to read, and kept pointing him to Jesus.

During the course of our conversations over those few months, I saw Matt let go and let God deal with his wife, his marriage, and many of his life challenges. He started focusing on his relationship with Jesus. He also received some counseling from our pastor, who gave Matt the same message: get into a relationship with Jesus. When that relationship is right, then all the other stuff falls into place.

By late October that year Matt stopped calling as often, but when we did talk, I could tell immediately that he had changed. His circumstances weren't a whole lot better, but how he dealt with them certainly was. It was clear that Matt had fallen in love with Jesus. When everything seemed upside down, Matt found his anchor and knew that God had him. He would get upset about setbacks, but he had a peace about him and every time, he handed his troubles over to God.

I was in a life group at church with Matt's parents but didn't realize they were related until Matt's mom, Julie, came up to me that fall and thanked me for speaking with Matt. I told his parents that I was so excited to see what God was going to do with Matt. Matt was on fire for Jesus and there was no way you could be around him and not see that he was 'all in' with Jesus.

Then came that early morning call on January 1, 2016. Julie told me Matt was killed in an accident the night before. I can't even remember what I said to her, but my heart broke. Here was a young man who had finally found peace, who was on fire for God and now... he was gone. I can remember asking God, "Why?"

Little did I know how far Matt's Facebook post would reach and as I researched this story, what impact he had had on so many people in such a short period of time. As I look back on Matt's life, I am reminded of Isaiah 55: 8-9, "For My thoughts are not your thoughts, neither are your ways My ways, declares the Lord. As the heavens are higher than the earth, so are My ways higher than your ways and My thoughts than your thoughts." God has a plan; I may not understand it, but it's a good plan.

I know where Matt is and I'm a bit jealous that he is with God right now, but I will see him soon enough. I had a front row seat and watched God do some amazing things in Matt's life over a very short period of time. For most of us, it would take God years to do what he did in Matt's last six months. It was truly my honor to be part of his life here on this earth. I know Matt would hope that by sharing his story, you the reader, will find your level ground as he did—in Jesus Christ.

Skip Watkins

Chapter One

Light.

That was the last thing Matt DeRemer saw before he died—twin bright lights, from the headlights of a 2012 Lincoln sedan that turned left and straight into the path of Matt's motorcycle, hitting the former Marine head-on. Light was also the thing Matt loved most about life—seeing light in the world, being a light to others, and finding the light within himself. He did all of those things in the last few hours of 2015, with no idea the impact his death would have on total strangers.

It was a little before eight on a warm, clear New Year's Eve in 2015 when the car collided with Matt's bike. But what would have been a simple car crash, a tragic footnote in the next day's paper, went viral as Matt's last words and his story caught fire with the world. The impact of his life multiplied in the following hours, days, and weeks—all because of a simple Facebook message. In life, Matt was a flickering light to all who knew him, but in death he became a beacon to thousands looking for hope.

He'd returned home to Florida eighteen months earlier and, as 2015 drew to a close, Matt was finally feeling hopeful, feeling a peace that he never really had before. He set out on his motorcycle, heading for his parents' house in Seminole. His life had been uneven for most of his thirty-one years, and six months earlier he had gone to a local church in despair. His marriage was breaking up, the plans he'd made for his life were falling apart, and he was looking for somewhere to turn. Someone to turn to.

The former Marine had battled bipolar disease most of his life, but hadn't been diagnosed until he was an adult. The erratic nature of his mind often warred with the dreams he had for his future, and with his own best intentions. The disease had broken up relationships, cost him jobs, and gotten him hurt. Anyone who knew him would say it also made him one of the most compassionate, warm, and loving people in the world. He had a smile that could light up a room and a personality that exploded out of his Facebook posts, his letters and his conversations.

He was excited about Christmas and being with his family, but at the same time, Matt was still searching for what he wanted his life to be going into 2016. That morning, he'd posted on Facebook, communicating with the hundreds of people he'd met over his lifetime. People who loved him, people who helped him, and people who had been impacted by his presence.

Last day of 2015!!!!! For me I'll be meditating through all I do, on this entire year. I've lost, I've gained, family closer and tougher than ever before, loved ones lost, and new friends found. There has been many times where I've been found on my knees in prayer for hours (relentless) and other times leading a group of people in prayer, my faith (that I love to share) is an everyday awakening (to me) that people, lives, and circumstances can change for the better OVERTIME. I look back at 2015's huge challenges that I've overcome, shared with others, and have once again found myself...

To say thank you and bring on 2016, much work to be done!

He posted a meme with a quote from his favorite book, *Just One Day*, by Gayle Forman: "We are born in 1 day. We die in 1 day. We can change in 1 day. And we can fall in love in 1 day. Anything can happen in 1 day."

And then he posted one more sentence, unaware how prophetic his words would be, how they would bring tens of thousands of people together and open a dialogue about bipolar disease, and life, and God. "I don't really know where I'll end up tonight," Matt posted, "but I do know where I wind up is where I am meant to be."

Ten hours later, Matt DeRemer, who loved Christmas lights and donuts and prime rib, was hit by an alleged drunk driver in Largo, Florida. He'd just turned thirty-one a few days earlier and was poised to start the New Year with a new job as a surgical technician and a new faith in God. It was the change he'd been praying for and seeking; and just when he had that glimpse of a bright future, it was taken away.

His life had not been easy. He was born December 26, 1984, the second of two children to a hardworking Midwestern family. Matt, his sister Lynsey, and his parents Michael and Julie, lived in Fort Wayne for most of his childhood. A normal American family—Mom working at a hospital, Dad running his own water conditioning company, the two kids acting like all other siblings, playing together one second and bickering the next.

Matt was always loud and outrageous, the exact opposite of quiet, calm Lynsey. He loved anything that lit up or moved. As a baby, he wanted to be rocked, to sit in the bouncy seat, to do everything that was the opposite of still. Even as a toddler, Matt was particular about his things and liked specific toys, clothes, and shoes. When his mother tried potty training, Matt couldn't be swayed by any type of underwear. He wanted a certain kind of GI Joe-themed underwear. His mother scoured the local stores until she finally found the exact ones Matt wanted. That was all it took for him to leave diapers behind.

Matt was called hyperactive when he was little, but his parents chalked that up to him being a normal boy with maybe a little more energy than other boys his age. When his first preschool kicked him out for being overly challenging, his parents found one more suited to their energetic, slightly mischievous boy.

Today, Matt might have been labeled ADHD, but back then the diagnosis wasn't as common and the outside world just saw him as a boy who needed discipline. What other people didn't realize was how much time and effort Matt's parents put into giving their son direction and outlets for his energy. They tried everything—enrolling him in sports, keeping him active, eliminating sugars and dyes from his food—and though those things helped some, Matt was still an energetic, curious, impish boy.

"Back then, you didn't put a label on behavior like that," Julie said. "You just dealt with it. We didn't have all the resources that are available today. So we just talked to him, watched over him, and prayed with him."

Matt was the kind of kid, his mom said, who couldn't be told the stove was hot. He had to test the stove, and test all the boundaries around him. He was four when he lit his grandmother's dining room chair on fire—not out of malice, but because he was curious to see how fire worked. His parents took him to the fire station and, along with a tour of the fire trucks, Matt got a peek inside what happens when a fire rages out of control. Because he was bright and compassionate, that lesson stuck with him. Even at that young age, he made the connection and never set anything on fire again.

He loved to read and to experience the world. From the day he was born, he was hungry to try things, to take chances, to stretch his wings. When he was in second grade, his father pulled him out of school for a couple of days and took him to Colorado to visit his uncle. The uncle had a 182 Cessna Turbo four-seater plane. After taking off, his uncle asked him if he wanted to fly it. Matt was too short to reach the foot pedals, but he grabbed hold of the yoke and guided the plane through the skies over Denver.

When he got back to school, he told his teacher he had flown a plane. Matt was a kid full of imagination and stories and the teacher didn't believe him. Yet, it was that quality that made him unique among his friends.

He learned early on that he could captivate an audience with an outrageous story, and the older he got, the more outrageous the stories became. He spent so much time in his head that he earned the nickname 'Dreamer', something that stuck with him into adulthood.

He was close to his mother and sister, but not so much his father in those early years. With his mother, Matt would lay on her bed and talk for hours. They had a close bond, and for most of his life, Matt would turn to his mother first for advice about finances, girls, or life. With Lynsey, Matt took on a protective role when he was older, standing up to some kids who bullied her. He loved his family fiercely, and told them so often.

Mike didn't have those hours with Matt that Julie had, and that impacted his relationship with his son. Mike worked a lot when Matt was little, so when Matt was ten, Mike started taking him hunting and fishing as a way to bond with his son.

In the woods or by a quiet stream, Matt had long conversations with his father. They traipsed over fallen logs, aimed their rifles at lightning-quick squirrels, and began to build the connection they would need when Matt became an adult and lost his tether to his family for a while.

Mike, an enthusiastic outdoorsman, often competed in compound bow shooting competitions. One time, he brought Matt along to a competition. Matt wanted to try the sport, so Mike bought his son a cheap double-limbed compound bow. It didn't have sights or any of the fancy gear that the pros used, but it was something for Matt to try.

Matt, bright and quick to learn, managed to shoot well enough that day to qualify for the national kids' level championships. Mike was stunned. His novice son, with virtually no practice and a bargain bow, wanted to go to the competition and go up against some of the best archers in the world. "You can't change my destiny, Dad," Matt said when Mike hesitated. "You have to take me."

So the two of them loaded up Mike's camper and drove to Illinois. When they arrived, Mike saw the other kids with their dogged determination and professional equipment. Mike bought his son a set of matching arrows to replace the ones he'd cobbled together for the other competition, then pulled Matt aside before the match started. "I want you to shoot the best you can," his father said, "and leave it lie like that."

Matt did exactly what his father said. Although he didn't come in the top three, he placed high in the group of fifty kids there, and kept pace with several very skilled archers. "You didn't win," Mike told his disappointed son, "but you beat a lot of those kids. I couldn't even beat some of them. I'm proud of you."

As an adult, Matt picked archery up again while living in California, fresh out of the military and dealing with his bipolar diagnosis. The archery, he found, required focus and patience. Stillness. For those split seconds between sighting and releasing the arrow, Matt could find calm in his head.

When Matt was living in California, his father sent him one of his best compound bows, thrilled that his son was interested in the sport again. Matt used that bow over and over again, and after his death, Mike took it home. He still hasn't been able to bring himself to pick it up, to place his hands where his son's once rested and release an arrow into the air. Still, the day he watched his little boy compete against the best archers in the nation remains a beloved memory.

All his life, Matt was restless; always moving, always looking for the next thing. As a child, there weren't enough football practices or days in the woods to tame the constant energy inside him. His parents supported every activity he and Lynsey signed up for, and sometimes spent more time in their conversion van shuttling the kids from practice to practice than they did at home.

Matt played soccer, baseball, and basketball, but as he got older, the difference between him and the other kids became more pronounced. He had difficulty concentrating. He struggled to make lasting friendships. His moods fluctuated from one day to the next, sometimes one minute to the next.

In Matt's mind, the world was either moving too fast for him to latch onto or it wasn't moving fast enough to keep up with all he wanted to do. He struggled to pay attention and to remember the hundreds of things any kid in school needs to do, so he began to make lists, something he did up until the day he died. He'd forget about a project until the last second, then stress that it wasn't perfect, obsessing over every last detail.

He went to church on Sunday with his family, played pee-wee football, managed to hold As and Bs in school, but there was always something missing in Matt, some quest to be more. He didn't know it then, but part of that quest involved finding God, discovering who Matt was in God's eyes. It would take him several more states and two more decades to find those answers. And when he did, he made it his mission to tell the world one last, big, outrageous story of a life lived out loud.

Chapter Two

New Year's Eve—the night we say goodbye to old habits and hello to new beginnings. The DeRemers felt optimistic that night because their family was coming back together, filling in the holes that had built up over the last few difficult years.

The grandfather clock against the wall of the DeRemer living room ticked past 7:30. Matt's mother had made dinner—stone crab claws, steak, a decadent dessert—and the whole family was waiting for Matt to arrive before they ate together. It was a New Year's Eve family tradition—a meal together, followed by a few hours of playing board games like Apples to Apples and Uno, and catching up before the new year dawned.

Earlier, Matt had texted his mother to say he was running late because he had some laundry to do. Julie and Mike waited and the food grew cold. By 8:30, Matt still hadn't shown up. They decided to go ahead and eat, but Mike barely tasted his food. His gut churned with that sixth sense that all parents have...

Something was very, very wrong.

Lynsey offered to drive over to Matt's apartment and check on him, and upon arriving discovered he wasn't there. He hadn't called, hadn't texted, nor had he answered his parents' calls. The DeRemers stayed up late, leaving the front porch light on and the door unlocked. Julie changed into her pajamas but Mike couldn't fall asleep. He simply could not shake that feeling of unease.

A little after ten o'clock, the doorbell rang—a bad, bad sign. Matt would have walked in unannounced. Anyone who rang the doorbell at that time of night brought news no one wanted to hear.

But still they hoped that maybe Matt had been in an accident or his motorcycle had broken down. Matt had been in a hit-and-run accident on his bike a few months earlier, but after a short hospital stay, he was fine. Both Mike and Julie hoped for the same this time.

A Florida State Trooper stood on their porch, tall and stern and unsmiling. The same light that was left on to be a welcoming beacon for Matt now cast a shadow beneath the dome of the officer's green, wide-brimmed hat.

The trooper stood there a moment, finding his words, and in the space of that silence, Mike and Julie already knew their world would never be the same again. The trooper asked for their IDs, and Julie asked if she should get dressed first, thinking they were just going to the hospital. Mike, however, had seen the look in the trooper's eyes, and knew there was no reason to rush out the door.

The trooper spoke the words no one wants to deliver and grief hit the DeRemers in one hard, fast sucker punch, the kind of pain no one can describe and no one can understand, unless they have been there themselves. Matt, their bright light and their only son, was gone.

Mike and Julie were understandably angry. They had few details and felt powerless, lost. They went to the morgue to try and see Matt's body but the coroner wouldn't let them in, most likely to spare the family additional pain. Julie went home and sat in front of the computer, refreshing Facebook over and over again. As the news began to spread across the site, Matt's friends filled in some of the blanks about Matt's final hours. "Around three in the morning, the police brought us a bag with just his shoes in it. I wanted to know where everything else was," Julie said. "Where was everything else?"

But more, where was her son? The hole Matt left in his wake was deep, bottomless. The young boy who had been so loud left behind a heartbreaking silence the family could never fill again.

After that night, the biggest question the DeRemers had was *what do we do from here?* How did they begin to recover from the tragic loss of their beloved son, and how did they keep his memory alive? It seemed unfair that someone who lived so large and out loud should be reduced to a few paragraphs in the obituary section of the *Tampa Bay Times.*

Matt had already unwittingly done some of that work with his New Year's Eve Facebook post. When Matt's friends learned of his death, they began to share his post, moved by the irony and depth of his message: *I don't really know where I'll end up tonight, but I do know where I wind up is where I am meant to be.*

Friends of theirs shared it. Perfect strangers shared it. And then Ashton Kutcher saw the post on Twitter and sent it out to his hundreds of thousands of followers. A week after his death, Matt DeRemer had gone viral.

The next thing the family knew, the local news stations and then all the national networks and media, like *Good Morning America* and CNN, were standing on their doorstep or calling constantly, all wanting to hear Matt's story. It seemed the world wanted to understand what had brought him peace on his last day. To take a peek inside the life of a man who had died too young. What no one really knew was how difficult that journey had been for Matt.

The constant energy that was a part of his childhood stayed with Matt into his teen years and adulthood. It was part of what drove everyone around him crazy, but also part of what made him so friendly and likable and popular, and why there were so many hundreds of brokenhearted people after his passing.

By the time of his death, Matt had made friends all over the country, and was rebuilding friendships that he'd made in Florida as a teenager. In the year 2000, the family had moved from Fort Wayne to Florida. Years earlier, they had visited Indian Rocks Beach on vacation and fell in love with the area. Mike sold his business and the whole family settled into life in the Sunshine State. Lynsey went to a Christian high school but Matt opted for the public school, primarily because he was interested in their sports programs.

The family was active at Indian Rocks Baptist Church, but Matt, like many teenagers, wasn't interested in what he saw as the shackles of religion. He wanted to live his life and experience a new world. Matt went to church with his family and knew all the right words, but wasn't ready to let God be God in his life.

On his first day of high school, he met Rick Brumett and Julio Caballero, who would become lifelong friends. The three of them were typical high schoolers—pulling crazy pranks, like running naked through the golf course's sprinklers in the dark. Matt had a constant energy about him and liked to be surrounded by people. It gave him comfort, acceptance, and fed his need to be liked. When he was in the happy phase of his bipolar condition, he was the center of attention. His favorite phrase, the one that sits beside the bio in his yearbook, was "Boom!" for *that's it, you've got it.* The word would explode out of him, loud and brash, then Matt would make a thumbs-up signal and give everyone his quirky, infectious smile.

Then the dark days would come and Matt would withdraw into himself, as if a shade had been drawn inside his mind. The bubbly, excited side of him would disappear for a few days, then just as suddenly resurface like a bear coming out of hibernation.

His friends got used to his highs and lows and chalked it up as part of Matt's personality. Rick and Julio nicknamed him 'Dreamer' because Matt was always off in his own mental world. Just as quickly, his mood would shift and he'd be making a crowd of people laugh with his funny antics and faces. As Matt got older, his mood swings began to get wider and more pronounced, and started to negatively impact his relationships.

He knew, even when he was younger, that there was something "off". He knew he didn't act or react like those around him. He called the manic times "the Mad Hatter taking over" and knew that those moments, when his reality was distorted, caused arguments. "Home," he wrote in his journal years later while away at boot camp, "is a place where my illusions began of what life, love, happiness, sadness, pain, and knowing myself began... My home is a place where growing up tangled within our complicated drama is a place I yearn for."

Maybe it was insecurity or maybe it was part of his disease, but Matt had a tendency to smother people. He tried too hard, his friends said, focusing incessantly on one girl and the quest to win her over. To find the love and acceptance he searched for his whole life. Rick and Julio loved Matt, but even they would pull away from him when Matt became needy and clingy. That same tendency to go big with his adventures and his stories became part of his relationships, especially with women.

In his sophomore year, Matt met a girl named Jessie and dated her until they started junior college and she reconnected with an old boyfriend. Their breakup devastated him. They had spent nearly every day together and Matt truly believed she was the love of his life. Their relationship was filled with the same roller coaster as Matt's mind—crazy highs and deep, dark lows. When he was depressed, there was no convincing him things would get better. And when he was manic, the world became his playground.

He would push too much, people said. Take a joke a little too far or draw out a conversation a little too long. It alienated people, leaving Matt alone, and the cycle of finding people, winning them over and making sure they loved him would begin anew. Matt flitted from group to group, never quite fitting in or finding his place.

Over the course of his life, Matt kept several journals, often writing prayers and wishes for his future, as if inking them on the college-ruled pages would make them come true. "I am asking for friends," he wrote to God, "of like minds, similar pasts, life-altering wisdom and life-altering bonds. I feel like an alien!"

And maybe he was one. An alien with a disease no one around him understood. An alien with a brain that was never predictable, never settled. An alien who was lost and stumbling from one place to the next, searching for his peace. Yet, he persevered, because if there was one thing Matt DeRemer didn't believe in, it was quitting, even if going forward meant getting hurt.

When Matt was five years old, he took the training wheels off his bike and promptly crashed because he didn't know how to stop. His parents thought that would slow him down and offered to put the training wheels back on, but Matt said no. He got back on his bike the next day, falling and getting up over and over again until he had the two-wheeler under control.

It was the same with his disease. He fell and got up, over and over again, in a daily battle to keep the warring factions of his mind under control. The only thing that seemed to settle him was sticking to a routine and writing lists, something he discovered in high school. Like everything else in Matt's life, what brought him peace came at a price.

Chapter Three

If there was one place where Matt could quiet the voices in his head and find some measure of peace, it was the gym. He started bodybuilding in high school. Like many things in his life, it became an obsession. The manic side of his bipolar disease was soothed by the punishing workouts. They'd exhaust him, require deep concentration, and let him sleep a little, but the manic side took as much as it gave. When he was on that upswing, Matt was exuberant, obsessive, and hyper-focused.

The evidence of how obsessed he was with bodybuilding was clear in his journals. He detailed every supplement he took, every exercise, and every repetition. He poured over the numbers, analyzing, tweaking, and shifting. He read everything he could, talked about his workouts with everyone who would listen, and chronicled all of it in thick notebooks.

When he was older, he built a website named *Fat to Freak*, dedicated to his bodybuilding. On there, he wrote, "I grew up in a neighborhood where all the kids had some kind of talent. May it be at basketball, football, running, soccer, or all of them together, I fell short of being able to play alongside of them because I really didn't find my talents till later. Moving on....I moved from the state I grew up in to another very competitive state where all the kids that surrounded me were super athletes. I tried the best I could and just never fulfilled any real monumental ground-breaking discoveries. That's until I found bodybuilding."

His friends joined him in the gym, but none of them pushed it as hard and fast as Matt did. His insecurity about his looks only fueled his focus to create the perfect body. "I have always wanted to be a super freak," he wrote on the site. "I have always wanted to be the biggest kid on the block."

He found like minds in the latter part of his high school years. "[They] taught me the art of pain, devotion, determination, and competition. Also, they taught me how to destroy myself in the gym and over time the feeling became a high. Plus, there is nothing like the rage you can release from a battle in the gym. I found my talent in this one team sport, the only person that can make or break your dreams is yourself."

To get to where he wanted to be, he ramped up his supplement usage, maxing out his testosterone levels at 1100 ng/dl. The increasingly challenging workouts also helped sooth his depression and take the edge off the manic days. Then someone would reject him or he'd lose a friend, or have trouble with his girlfriend, and he would turn to the gym, working out harder as a solution.

That hyper-focus is common in people with bipolar disorder. Matt had that hyper-focus with the people in his life, particularly women, and with whatever his passion was at the time. He'd become so focused he would exclude everyone and everything else. It was like one of those cameras you use to view an eclipse—everything in his world would narrow to that one tiny pinprick hole. It made the people around him crazy.

He would drive people away and then bring them back, a boomerang that echoed the swings in his moods. On the outside, Matt seemed fun and energetic, always smiling and anxious to get started, to get involved. On the inside, he felt lost—misunderstood and unloved—which left him at odds with others and with himself.

He was on the wrestling team in high school, a sport that he thoroughly enjoyed. Like many of the activities he participated in, wrestling required tough workouts, single-minded determination, and a strong focus in the moment. His coaches were extremely tough on him. Their constant criticism made Matt feel defeated and worthless. One afternoon, he and Jessie bought a couple cans of spray paint and plastered all the negative words and names the coaches had called him on the walls of his room. Matt wasn't a kid who got in trouble in school or got in fights, but he was a kid who felt every one of those verbal arrows deep in his soul.

His mother came home and saw her son's heartbreak scrawled in massive letters on his walls. She didn't reprimand him and didn't ground him. Instead, she told her son that she saw and understood his pain. "Wow," she said, and drew her boy into a hug. "You had a rough day."

Matt gave his mother that unflappable grin. "I was out of paper," he said, "so I sort of blew up at my room."

Matt struggled with his faith, with the restrictions of the church and his parents. Like he did with the bodybuilding, he journaled and wrote, trying to understand his world and what was going on inside his head. He was frustrated and lost, and coupled with the angst and emotional volatility of his teenage years, Matt struggled daily to make sense of what he was going through. And maybe in a bit of prophetic thinking, he wrote a poem about his battle, saying that only death could free him from it, even though he knew how painful that loss would be to his family.

Running from the past
Knowing that things will never last!
The madness of all the questions,
Awaiting the same stupid suggestions,

Living to no one's surprise!
Hiding from voices that come to terrorize.
Waiting for silence from the world,
Suddenly all the answers become unfurled!

Existing only on fate
All because of being born to a world a little too late!
To me nothing is fair.
All I've got left is God and a simple prayer.

From the past I run
Because nothing was said or done.
Looking upon my death,
Taking my final breath!

For here you see,
This is the only way to be free!

My only fear,
Is seeing my loved one's shedding a tear!

I see wasted screams
And think of all the painful screams!
For I have nothing to regret
Because I'm at no threat!

Running from my past
Knowing that things will never last!
The madness of all the questions,
Awaiting the same stupid suggestions!

As high school came to an end, Matt's structured world began to spiral out of control. He constantly argued with his parents about rules and restrictions. At one point, the arguments were so bad his father wrote him a letter rather than speaking face-to-face.

His parents did their best to steer Matt in the right direction, but teen rebellion, coupled with his as yet undiagnosed bipolar disease, made it difficult to corral him. His father tried to use the logic of Christianity to get through to Matt. In his letter, he talked about God's rules for living a good life and how embracing or ignoring those rules had a negative impact. Mike emphasized the importance of holding a job, keeping a positive attitude, and focusing on helping others. He closed the letter by advising Matt to look to God, because He was waiting for Matt to turn in His direction. Maybe if Matt had taken that message to heart earlier, an entire chain of events could have been avoided. He wasn't ready, and though he loved his parents, he was determined to make his own path and to live life on his own terms.

Around this time, Matt's relationship with Jesse was beginning to deteriorate and his two best friends, Rick and Julio, had enlisted in the Marines. Matt opted to enter the Certified Nursing Assistant program at a local junior college, the same one his girlfriend was attending. He got a job at a hospital but quickly realized he didn't like it and didn't want to go into that field as a lifetime career.

When his girlfriend came back from vacation and told him she had gotten back together with her ex-boyfriend, the Jenga stack that was Matt's life fell apart. In a rather short period of time he received four speeding tickets, as well as a reckless driving citation. He was lost and floundering around, looking for something to cling to.

He found that when he went to Parris Island, North Carolina, to see Julio's graduation from the Marine Corps boot camp. The boys he knew from high school, who pulled pranks and ducked responsibilities, had become men. Tall, proud, respectful, driven men. Matt looked around the base and saw the same everywhere—young men who had their lives under control, who knew what their next step would be. Young men who built a family from their fellow Marines, their camaraderie a secret code that only those who have been Marines truly understand.

In that moment on the base, Matt thought he had found what he was looking for—the place where he could fit and flourish. He believed in the values of the Marines: Honor, Courage, Committment. The obsessive, focused part of Matt felt that structure might just be the answer to the frenetic pace in his head.

So he came home and, in typical Matt spontaneity and leap-before-you-look fashion, he walked into a recruitment office and enlisted with the Marines. At the time, he had no idea how that one oath would change him in deep, fundamental ways—but also give him the tools to finally understand himself.

A few days later, he sat down with his parents at the dining room table and announced his enlistment. Not that he'd looked into it or met with a recruiter, but that it was a done deal. He'd never mentioned wanting to join before and the news threw his parents for a loop. "I'm just frustrated with all the rules you have here," Matt said.

"Well, I'm sure the Marines don't have any rules," his father joked.

His father then asked Matt if he was aware that he'd joined the military during war time. "They're going to send you to the worst places because you are new and young," Mike said, desperate to get through to his son even though he knew the decision was already made and the contract inked. "Do you know where the safest place in the world is, Matt?"

Matt shook his head.

"That's probably where you want to be, isn't it?"

Matt nodded.

"The safest place in the world is in God's will," Mike said. "But you aren't in God's will, you're in Matt's will. If you're in God's will, it doesn't matter if a thousand people are shooting at you, you're not going to be hit. You need to get in God's will, Matt."

Matt assured his father that he understood, but it wasn't until he was in Fallujah, surrounded by fire fights and danger and death, that the lesson finally sank in. By then, he was already the property of the U.S. government, and leaving wasn't an option.

Chapter Four

Fallujah.

That's where Matt found himself a few months after boot camp. Smack dab in the middle of the second Gulf war in hot, dusty, dangerous Fallujah, Iraq—amidst, as his father warned, some of the worst fighting.

Basic training at Parris Island was twelve weeks of hell. His drill instructor criticized him for being lazy, fat, and not worth the ground he walked on. In his journal, Matt admitted the drill instructor was right. "I've been holding back because I'm not sure about anything…I know I'm lazy and need this, but how will it help if I don't let the process in? Seriously, only God can decide. He's the only thing that can help me in life."

Matt began to work harder, became comfortable with a rifle, ran the confidence obstacle course over and over until he mastered it, and adapted to the regimented, ordered life of the Marine Corps. The fifty-four hours of Crucible training—a non-stop, constant barrage of activities on little sleep and little food—nearly broke him, but taught him the importance of his unit. Of working together with others.

All these skills would serve him well when he was dropped into a war zone with the 2nd Battalion, 7th Marine Regiment. He spent a few more months in training, learning how to operate trucks and Humvees and how to deal with the arid desert conditions. He was promoted to Lance Corporal and thought he had it all together, that he knew what to expect. He was wrong.

Fallujah was as hot as the deepest regions of the sun, with temperatures reaching 115 degrees during the day. The air was dry, the kind of dry that sucked the strength right out of a man. Everything was covered in sand, without the benefit of the ocean Matt was so used to seeing in Florida. He learned quickly to stay hydrated and to grab catnaps whenever he could.

He was assigned to one of the riskiest jobs in the Marines—driving a truck full of supplies to other units. Since it was safer for the convoys to drive at night, under cover of darkness, most of his runs were after sundown. He'd get behind the wheel of a seven-ton truck, loaded with men and replenishments, and hit the increasingly dangerous roads. IEDs (Improvised Explosive Devices) littered the roads, requiring drivers to be alert and aware every single second.

It was an overwhelming, terrifying introduction to life as a Marine. Matt's hyper-focus tendencies helped and hurt him in the military—it would come in handy in being organized and detailed, but at the same time, his quest for perfection would almost paralyze him. He routinely beat himself up for the smallest of mistakes, and begged God to change him. "I see the error of my ways. The lying, cursing, stealing…I hope God will see change in me and provide me with the will and the future to graduate with my platoon! This is all I have and the only thing I want is to be around people with the same goals and life."

In a war zone, there was no room for being depressed or swinging into a manic state. The Marines expected dependable, consistent performance from him every single day. It was a lot for Matt to handle; far, far more than he expected, and the pressure on him was enormous.

He lived for the breaks in the monotony. He played pranks on his friends, like the time he offered to give a fellow Marine a "trim" haircut and shaved his head instead as a joke. The care packages from home, filled with letters and favorite snacks, both calmed him and made him ache for all that he had left behind.

He wrote long letters to his family, pouring out the thoughts running through his head. What scared him, what he missed, what he was going through. He included pictures, which gave his parents on the other side of the world some peace of mind.

He kept the day-to-day terror mostly to himself. The stories of running over an IED that detonated, blew off the passenger's side door, and knocked Matt out for several minutes. The near-misses that left them all jittery and grateful. The firefights that scared them all and kept them on edge, the constant rattle of gunfire, along with the disturbing smell of things burning in the distance were only spoken about in hushed tones long after he'd come home.

Matt loved the convoy group he was with, loved the way the drives broke up the monotony of life on base. For the first time, he felt part of a group. And most of all, he loved fellow Marine Garcia, who had become a close friend.

"He was my rock," Matt wrote in his journal. "He was a light to get a sense of wellness and a sense of direction from. He was someone to remember. Hidden underneath was a person that I have always wanted to be and a person I have always wanted to be around. He was a symbol of a better life because [with Garcia around], I would see things differently than I see them now."

Everything changed for Matt in the early morning hours of July 2, 2007. He was in a supply convoy returning from a successful run, with Garcia in the truck behind him. "This day was like all the others," Matt wrote. "Wake up mid-day, check weapons, check truck before convoy heads out, check gear." The road back, however, had been altered, and Matt said he got a little jumpy because he felt like the space was too exposed. Garcia's truck hit an IED that Matt's truck missed. The bomb exploded in a blinding flash and it was instant chaos. Seconds were minutes, Matt wrote, and minutes felt like hours. Then the radio crackled with the words, "Garcia is down!"

The IED had ripped off the back half of Garcia's truck and crumpled the wheel well armor plate into the driver's seat, crushing Garcia into the cramped space.

"When the explosion happened," Matt wrote, "my mind changed from an obeying Lance Corporal to a man." Matt tried to jump out of his truck to help his friend. Matt was crying, hysterical, and he fought his NCO, who hauled him back and ordered him to stay put. His friend, the guy who had made him laugh and entertained so many of them on those long, hot days and nights, was pinned and dying. Matt forgot about the rest of the convoy, forgot about possible enemies lying in wait for just such an opportunity. He couldn't focus on anything other than the gasping, pleading, dying man behind him.

The sergeant could see the big picture—the other Marines' lives who were at risk, while they were stopped on the side of a wide, open road. Garcia was as good as dead, but the other men didn't have to join him. A helicopter took Garcia to the hospital, but it was too late and he died en route.

Matt did as he was ordered, but that moment was a turning point. In those seconds, he didn't see or understand the risk his fellow Marines were facing. All he saw was his friend, left to die in his truck. Joining the Marines had suddenly gone from an adventure to a hellish torture he just wanted to escape.

He questioned his reasons for being in Fallujah. He questioned a God who could let a good man like Garcia die in such a horrific way. He questioned everything he thought he knew. Most of all, he questioned himself. In a psychiatric evaluation, Matt's doctor wrote, "...he has guilt over causing his friend's death, which he feels was secondary to his tripping the wire, causing the explosion that killed his friend."

Garcia's death plunged Matt into a deep, dark depression. He dropped into that pit and had an almost impossible time climbing out of it. In his journals, Matt wrote about feeling like an empty shell, like he had no purpose in life. The military, which he had looked at as a positive way to change his life, had become a prison—and he desperately wanted out.

Chapter Five

The downward spiral that began with Garcia's death persisted throughout the remainder of his tour in Fallujah and lingered when Matt returned to the States. These dark months marked the first clear signs of his bipolar disease and the personal damage those lows left in their wake. Matt spent a short time in California, got into an on-again, off-again relationship with a woman named Tiffany, and managed a visit with his family before he was shipped off to Camp Hanson in Okinawa. Set apart from his original battalion, his family, and his girlfriend, Matt flailed around, trying to find where he fit in, trying to find something to hold on to, but was losing his grasp on himself more each day. Over and over, he called the people in his life, many of which were unanswered, most likely because there were times when Matt was too much to take. Even he acknowledged in his journal that his behavior was borderline stalking, especially when it came to Tiffany.

His family was on the other side of the world, watching Matt's descent into a deep, almost debilitating depression, and worried half out of their minds. Email exchanges would go in waves, with Matt pouring out his heart, then withdrawing and not answering for days. He'd argue with Tiffany, and then feel powerless to fix their relationship because of the great distance between them. He'd talk about breaking up, then a few hours later, be elated because they had talked and things were okay again. Just as quickly, the relationship would go south, taking Matt's emotions along for the ride.

He began talking to a psychiatrist on base. "At the time, he presented with symptoms of depression, emotional numbing, volatility, irritability and a decrease in his need for sleep along with pressured thinking and action," the doctor wrote in his report. "He spoke about fears of being alone, about mood swings into depression. He experienced frequent suicidal ideation but never wished to act upon these thoughts due to his religion. He also struggled with low self-esteem and hopelessness. He hated being in the Marines and having to perform the duties expected in his military obligation."

In July of 2008, a year after Garcia's death, Matt was teetering on a dark edge. "I am not suicidal," he wrote to his mother, "but I just feel like hurting myself to relieve the pain I am suffering. Working out till I blackout in the gym isn't working anymore. [Tiffany] doesn't understand that without her, I will feel nothing, I will not be in touch with anything anymore. I feel like I am nothing and I never will be."

He wrote about being alone, about how he felt like he was on the last of his nine lives. He struggled to stay positive, but the depression and despair he felt over his life and his relationship was almost impossible to overcome. He ends the email with one long plea: "Mom, mom, mom, mom, mom, mom, mom...........f*^@!"

Julie spent a sleepless night worrying about her son, writing back to him with advice and support. The next day, he was back and excited, sure that he had the answer for saving his relationship with Tiffany. In typical Matt fashion, he wanted to go big by finding the perfect piece of jewelry that would show her how much she meant and how committed he was. For days, he agonized over the purchase, searching the internet for the perfect gift, begging his mother to help him find something, so sure that it would be the key to making Tiffany happy again.

Then, just as quickly, his moods would spiral out of control. In retrospect, anyone reading his emails could see his manic waves were getting higher and his crashes lower. In August, he wrote his father: "Dad, it's really hard to talk about anything else except how much I have lost a firm grasp on reality. I can say right now that I don't really remember who I am or what I was about when people knew me. I am lost and my hole is bigger than I had thought."

Matt continued seeing the doctors on base, complaining about anxiety, insomnia, and trouble concentrating. The doctors gave him meds, told him it was PTSD, and sent him back to his quarters. Matt, however, knew it was more, that there was something else driving his pain. "I really do feel alone because no one knows why I am the way I am...I am losing a battle of sanity. I am my worst enemy and he is beating me to death with all these thoughts, nightmares, and everything I don't want to know about. I am just losing it."

The psychiatrist wrote that Matt "often felt his head was full of thoughts, then he would talk so fast he could not get the words out in a way that others could understand them. This was helped by Seroquel. He also spoke of detachment and of panic attacks, along with anxiety on a chronic basis."

He kept going to the doctors for help, tried different medications and therapies, and visited with the base Chaplin, seeking answers for his increasing mood swings. Severe shin splints restricted his gym activity, which meant he didn't have that endorphin release to help combat some of the depression.

He began to act out and blow up, which led to reprimands and restrictions. He had few friends, and being restricted to base made him even more isolated from his fellow Marines. He filled the pages of his journals, trying to figure his life and himself out. When he began to spiral down again, the tone of his emails would change and they would be riddled with spelling mistakes and run-on sentences. Even though he would ignore his parents' emails from time to time, he would freak out if they didn't reply right away, sending one with just this as the subject line: AS SOON AS YOU GET MY EMAILS, ANSWER THEM BEFORE I GO CRAZY AND LOSE MY SHIT!

Tiffany was back home in the United States and Matt was getting more and more desperate to hold onto her. He burned through phone cards and kept sending her emails and gifts. He wrote about what would happen if their relationship ended, alluding to hurting himself. "I know I will put myself in harm's way if that ever happens."

His heartsick parents talked to a doctor at the Veterans Affairs hospital in Florida, trying to figure out what was wrong with their son. “We love you and we want you back from all this,” his mother wrote. Powerless and desperate, all the DeRemers could do was keep talking to Matt and pray for God’s protection and help.

At the end of August, his psychiatric issues forced the military to send him home early from Okinawa, and the doctors finally formally diagnosed him with bipolar disorder. The diagnosis meant he was now considered disabled and no longer the soldier he’d wanted to be. The medical evaluation report laid out Matt’s awful new reality: *No access to weapons. No overnight duty. No field ops. No deployment. No heavy equipment operations.*

The diagnosis was devastating. “I contemplate slitting my throat every day. Even though I need to find myself, I need some kind of angel to come out somewhere and get me back to life before I ruin it,” he wrote to his parents. “I know this isn’t what you want to hear, but this life really isn’t worth any of my time. Where is my guardian angel when I need him? Mom, I am at the bottom again, and, well, inch by inch, I am losing my sanity. One day I might meet the devil, because heaven isn’t sending an intervention.”

Chapter Six

Bipolar Disorder. Those two words completely changed Matt DeRemer's life. The diagnosis put a label on him and made a man already struggling with self-acceptance feel like he was even more alone. He found a video on *YouTube* about bipolar disorder and would show it to anyone who would watch, both trying to explain himself and push people away before they could reject him.

His separation paperwork from the military included the IED explosions as part of the underlying cause for his mental issues, which meant it was service-related, giving him both an honorable discharge and long-term disability benefits. "Evaluation of bipolar disorder, NOS; with cognitive disorder, and PTSD—referred to as bipolar affective disorder II, with mood variability between depressive and hypomanic states to a moderate degree; claimed as TBI (Traumatic Brain Injury), anxiety with depression, sleep disorder, memory loss—for Disability Evaluation System (DES) purposes and proposed entitlement to service connection for Department of Veterans Affairs benefits."

The IED that knocked him unconscious for five minutes and left him with a concussion, coupled with his depression, anxiety, and PTSD created a 'constellation of symptoms', the military wrote in their report. The doctors surmised his traumatic brain injury from that event exacerbated the underlying bipolar disorder. His December 2009 psychiatric exam said that Matt reported "recurrent and intrusive thoughts of traumatic events, with an exaggerated startle response. You are not interested in activities you used to like and you spend more time alone. You feel detached or estranged from others." Matt was deemed unfit for duty and was discharged from the Marines on March 30, 2009. He had to sign a paper saying he accepted the recommendation of the medical board and, just like that, his life as a Marine was over. Matt was suddenly thrust into a new reality stamped with a crushing diagnosis.

Bipolar disorder is a complicated disease, often misdiagnosed for years because it masks itself in more common ailments like depression, insomnia, and panic attacks. It's the sixth leading cause of disability worldwide and is found in three percent of the general population, with another three percent experiencing symptoms that put them on the bipolar disorder spectrum. Many people who suffer from bipolar disorder drink or do drugs to quiet their brains—Matt used alcohol and cigarettes on and off throughout the years.

Onset is often in puberty, with symptoms becoming full-blown in adulthood. The risk of suicide among sufferers is higher, and about thirty to forty percent of sufferers self-harm. Half of those with bipolar disorder experience delusions and hallucinations. They have trouble maintaining relationships, not just because the disease is so taxing for those around them, but because the bipolar part of their brain whispers untruths and doubts.

Rapid cycling is having more than four episodes a year, with a 'remission' of a couple of months between events. Some sufferers have one episode a year, others have several within a few weeks. The extreme mood swings go between a manic high and a depressive low. The manic episodes are characterized by an abnormally and persistently elevated mood with high bursts of energy and a limited need for sleep. The person has an inflated self-esteem, talks rapidly and is easily distracted, agitated and reckless. The depressive side of the disorder is marked by apathy, oversleeping, loss of energy, inability to concentrate or make a decision, suicidal thoughts, and a deep-rooted feeling of hopelessness. The symptoms for bipolar disorder are similar to those for schizophrenia, major depressive disorder, ADHD, and personality issues like borderline personality disorder.

Bipolar disorder is often treated two-fold, with both medications and psychotherapy. Working with a psychologist can help a sufferer recognize their episode triggers, reduce emotional suppression in relationships, and identify symptoms and implement coping mechanisms before a full-blown episode erupts.

Lithium, Carbamazepine, Ativan, Klonopin, Valproate, Lamotrigine, and other medications are used to treat bipolar disorder. The right combination is tailored to each patient, and doctors often go through months of trial and error before finding the perfect drug cocktail for symptom management. Bipolar disorder requires constant monitoring by a psychiatrist because there are side effects to each medication. Some patients build up tolerances and need to have their drug regimen adjusted, which can throw off their brain chemistry again. In addition, many patients start to feel better, convince themselves they are fine without the drugs, and go off them. Matt was one of those people. He hated the albatross of his diagnosis, and wanted to believe he could handle it on his own, as he had when he was younger.

The doctor's reports show the difficult time Matt had adjusting to the various drug therapies he was prescribed. Klonopin slowed his thought processes and allowed him to sleep, but left him 'unable to function'. Prozac acted like speed in his system, Trazodone made him too groggy the next day to work, and Depakote made him more irritable.

He was put on a combination of Lithium, Zyprexa and Ativan, which worked for quite a while. His Lithium dosage was quite high, and when Matt began to have side effects like weight gain, gastrointestinal issues, and exhaustion, he self-tapered his dose to half. The doctor noted that Matt's past steroid usage when he was bodybuilding and his occasional overindulgence in alcohol only made his bipolar disorder worse. "They can cause ongoing increased brain vulnerability to dysfunction."

In the months after the diagnosis, Matt struggled to accept the doctor's pronouncement, especially because his career in the Marines was, for all intents and purposes, over except for the paperwork. His worried family kept emailing him and talking to him, trying to keep him off the edge, but it was a daily battle. Julie and Mike spent many sleepless nights discussing their son.

"Everyone and everything has shown me that I am not for this world," Matt wrote. "I am done talking. Live your life and let this be. It is what it is." He wrote about sitting on the floor of his room, drunk, surrounded by bottles of pills. "I really want to lay in my bed and not wake up."

His mother wrote back in a panic, with emphasis and capital letters in her email. "ALL THESE THINGS are for someone to notice GOD is there with you. HE is telling you not to harm yourself or others. Matt, I CAN relate to you in the fact that many years of my life before you were born, I felt like my life was being wasted…It wasn't until I KNEW I HAD TO START OVER FRESH IN EVERY AREA OF MY LIFE that GOD put your dad into my life... Starting over is God's way of giving you a second chance... It sounds like you want a second chance, but are afraid before you reach out that it might not work out, either." She urged him to talk to God, to reach out to Him. To start going to counseling and trust that God had a plan. "Life is better with God than without God," she said.

There was no Hollywood revelatory moment that night, or any of the nights after that. Matt's acceptance of his disorder would be a long time coming, and the medications and therapy to help him cope didn't suddenly change his state overnight.

He was frustrated with the long wait between appointments and the duty restrictions that left him on base with nothing to do but stare at the walls. "All I need now is a pair of balls to do what I want to do and let me tell you…they are growing every day. Stop calling me, stop everything. I am gone. I am a ghost."

Chapter Seven

On and off—that became the theme for Matt's next few years. He'd go on and off his medications, on and off his relationships, and on and off his goals for his life. Perhaps a part of him was lost, cut adrift from the Marines, across the country from his family, and now burdened by a diagnosis that made him different from everyone he knew.

He was living in California at Camp Pendleton, waiting out the remaining days until his discharge was finalized. He spent hours in chat rooms for fitness buffs, connecting with people around the world, feeding his need for contact and for information. As he had in high school, he buried himself in information and workouts, consuming his days in the gym.

In February, he met a woman named Crissy who was in California on a clinical rotation and living with her brother. Matt and she agreed to meet at a gym and do a workout together. Matt was smitten from that first day. When he dropped her off, he didn't want to leave and convinced her to let him stay at her brother's house until

4 a.m., so he could make it back in time for the base curfew.

Six weeks later, Crissy had to return to school in Pennsylvania. Before she left, he took a chance and told her about the bipolar disorder. He wasn't sure how she would react, but Crissy, who had only known him on his meds, encouraged him to keep up with his medications and therapy and it would all be fine.

Except Matt didn't do that. Like many bipolar people, he grew confident when he was on a high and think he didn't need the medication. It wasn't until he dropped into the lowest of lows that he would see the flaw in that decision. Nevertheless, it was an on-again, off-again pattern that repeated dozens of times in the next few years.

In their time apart, Matt and Crissy emailed and called each other constantly. When she had to return for another clinical rotation in May, he flew out to Pennsylvania to drive back with her. Matt had been discharged that March and was floundering at the time, trying to figure out what he wanted to do with his future.

He was also struggling with Garcia's death. As the anniversary of that loss drew nearer, Matt's nightmares started increasing and, because he wasn't consistent about taking his medication, the trauma of his grief began to impact everything in his life. His journals and writings don't talk about his faith during this time, or whether he turned to God to help him cope, but they do show his wavering between despair and hope. He had enrolled in school to become a personal trainer, but the combination of school stress, Garcia's loss and the new relationship had Matt's moods swinging.

Crissy knew him at his rawest, his parents said, and her kindness and patience through the years they were together were a 'godsend'. She became very close with the family, emailing them and keeping them in the loop. After Matt's death, she stayed with Lynsey for a week. Matt was not an easy man to live with. He hated being left alone while Crissy was at school or work, and he struggled greatly with Crissy being more financially successful than he was. He became clingy and needy. For a young woman struggling to establish herself in medicine, Matt's constant pleas for attention were sometimes suffocating.

He started something in therapy called Stuck Point exercises. This focused on pinpointing the thoughts that kept him, essentially, stuck in an endless loop of negative thinking and anxiety. His therapist gave him worksheets to fill out where he identified an *Activating Event*, his *Belief or Stuck Point*, and any *Emotional Consequences.* Looking at these provides insight into the erratic nature of his mind and how it darted between elation and depression, sometimes in the course of a single day. Halloween 2009, for instance, reminded him of his family and of everyone he missed back home. That left him feeling sad. Then he took a test in school, did well, and was excited. An hour later, he did a sky dive jump, solo, and instead of making him happy, he noted feeling detached from his life, from everything. Then he saw Crissy and 'she saved the day', and Matt was happy.

When Crissy had an emotional crisis the next day, Matt was stunned that she was struggling and depressed. He said all he could do was hold her, but when asked what he felt about that, he said, "Blank."

It was Garcia his mind returned to, over and over again. His therapist had him write out an account of that day in Fallujah. Matt poured it all onto the page—the humdrum day before, the explosion, his reaction, the horror, scrawled in tight block letters on ten handwritten pages of a yellow legal pad.

The nightmares he'd only partly been able to keep at bay returned. He dreamed of Garcia's face, of the accident, then he would wake up screaming, sweaty, and panicked. "It's his face I see. For many years, that face had been a corpse. A corpse that stares at me, screams, and just burns. Pain, anger and sadness from him. And many prayers to give him his life, give him a second chance, from someone else's sacrifice (mine)."

Matt felt an overwhelming sense that he was letting his friend down. Every misstep, every bad grade, every argument with his family or Crissy, would spiral Matt back to thinking he was disappointing Garcia. He felt guilty that he had lived instead of his friend. "I'm betraying Garcia when I am wasting my time," Matt wrote. "I am failing at what needs to be done."

Dozens of times in his journals, in accounts of that day, Matt asked why he hadn't been the one killed. He felt an inordinate weight of responsibility to live up to Garcia's memory. "He should be here, not me. I am lazy. I just fill space. I am a waste of paste. People will never understand me. My life is pain, hatred, and sadness."

He wrote long, long pages about his memories of Garcia, and how that had opened his eyes to what was important in life. He wondered if the people around him would willingly give up a moment of happiness to avoid such a horrific event. That way they would never be subjected to the void Matt found himself lost in.

On his stressful days, or days when things went wrong, Matt said he could feel Garcia staring at him. "My memories of [Garcia] rarely go into who he was or how he acted, only how he left this planet. I am angry writing this and I admit I am thinking of how this just made me think of destroying anyone else's life that happiness progresses [through] on a daily basis," he wrote. "I am holding on just to hold on because the pain helps me get along in this world. Honestly, remembering his smile doesn't help me because all I do is cry when I think of it."

Around this same time, toward the last half of 2009, Crissy graduated from college and she and Matt moved in together. Until then, she didn't really know how often he was skipping his meds or how bad the bipolar disorder could get. When she realized all this, she threatened to leave him if he didn't stay on his medications and Matt stuck to that promise, for a while. Crissy passed her boards and the couple moved to San Ramon, California for her new job.

Matt didn't pass his physical trainer certification test, but Crissy encouraged him to stick with his schooling and try again. Money was tight—Matt would shop and spend like crazy when he was manic. Between his spending, their student loans, and the high cost of living in California, the two of them were constantly broke, which added to their fights and tension, as Crissy tried to encourage Matt to stay on track—with school, with finances, and with his medications.

He'd promise and fail, promise and fail. He'd get resentful at being told what to do and feel angry that his life was supposed to revolve around medications. He convinced himself he could control his moods on his own and told his parents he would only take the meds when he was overstressed. Crissy did her best to serve as an intermediary and to keep a positive attitude, but the fights between her and Matt began to take their toll.

Just before their trip to Florida for Christmas, Matt wrote an email to his mother. "Sorry for being an emotional buster [during] these times of joy. Days of new are coming and I can kind of see a light at the end of the tunnel." He talked about how he and Crissy had worked through a lot of their issues and that he was grateful for his parents being there to help him.

But behind the scenes, Matt was struggling with his self-worth, with his place in the world, and with the bipolar disorder that seemed to rule everything about him. He was only working part-time and often sank into depression in the hours he'd wait for Crissy to get home. It was only a matter of time before something gave and Matt's house of cards came tumbling down once again.

Chapter Eight

During the first half of 2010, the website, *Project: Fat to Freak* was Matt's newest passion. Matt ran into a friend at the gym earlier that year. The friend asked him what was wrong and why Matt had gained so much weight. For Matt, that was a wake-up call. He started the website to detail his transformation, and in the URL, called it *Dreamer Dreamin' Big.* "It was the end of the week and nothing but bad was all around me," Matt wrote on the site about that day he ran into his friend. "No good news. I happened to be in this gym I had just found, which happens to be a dying breed of hardcore gyms, and I was just destroying myself. The weights were getting heavier, the music in my ears could be heard from the front of the gym to the back, and the grunts were becoming louder (this is why I train late at night)."

His medications had caused him to gain a lot of weight and his motivation was sporadic at best (very likely related to his sporadic medication regimen). "Out of the many years I have trained myself and others, I have always fell short. I don't know if I need other trainers to keep me straight, but here are the problems: Too tired to get out of bed, cheating on the diet, late night wake-up calls to the kitchen, not completing the workouts that are tailored for the specific layer, and running short of funds to buy the gear I need."

He looked to the gym to save himself again—and like before, he became hyper-focused on everything that went into his body and every single rep he completed. He measured himself every Friday and would run out to the gym in the middle of the night if the numbers weren't what he wanted, frenetically working out to force a positive result. He would advise the readers of his site to be healthy and make good choices, but then admit to a semi-dangerous supplement pattern. "Due to being way out of shape, getting up to start the day is a chore: crawling to the bathroom, taking some uppers to [wake] me up, falling asleep in the shower till I burn myself due to the increasing [hot] water problem, and then I am ready to begin the day. After work when I'm heading to the gym, black powder is my savior to punish myself in the gym. I have learned that supplements aren't really necessary for a great workout, however I like to be crazy. Then, the recovery products and everything else to balance out this and that really brings a man down."

Matt's relationship with Crissy was also unbalanced. Their finances were out of control and she eventually took over the checkbook, putting Matt on a budget. She was working full time and he was looking for a job, which also fueled their stress and arguments. "I hurt so bad inside that my heart just went to flames," Matt wrote to his mother in an email. "Crissy just told me she needs a break, I'm a burden, and if I don't fix this, it's done. Sealed with a 'I'll always be there for you, love you, and hope you get your head out of your ass.' I'm motivated to find a job and see where I am headed because I feel truly alone."

He reminded his mother of some advice she had given him some months earlier, when she compared what he had been going through to drowning. "I'm underwater, about to run out of air," Matt said of how he was feeling just then, "and [Crissy] is worried I'm going to pull her down."

On top of that, he and his father had been arguing a lot. Their relationship had been strained for many years, and 2010 brought everything to a head. To be fair, Mike didn't understand bipolar disorder and thought his son just needed to get his act together. Mike also saw the constant barrage of emails and phone calls, many dragging Julie out of bed in the middle of the night, so she could talk to Matt until her son found his way back to center again. There was a prayer room at Indian Rocks School where Julie worked and she spent many hours on her knees, praying for guidance for her son and strength for their family.

Matt had always been very close to his mother, turning to her often for advice and support. His sister became a sounding board for his issues with Crissy, too. But when it came to Mike, there was a wall that kept the two apart. Matt missed his father and wanted so badly to bring the two of them together again. In the middle of the year, Matt sent his father an email, titled: 'DAD please read'.

When he was young, Matt and his father didn't have a lot in common. Mike loved fishing, camping, archery, and hunting—activities that were difficult for always-moving, hyperactive Matt to enjoy. Coupled with a parent who worked long hours trying to build a business, the bond between them was tenuous and fragmented easily. Matt told his father that part of what had kept him from making amends was that fragile connection. "I don't know how to communicate [with] you, understand your hobbies, and [I] still haven't found a middle ground for our conversations to lead to."

Earlier that week, Matt had realized the emotion swirling through him was anger. At first, he thought he was angry with his extended family, but he quickly realized it was about the lack of relationship with his father. "What if something happens to you," Matt wrote, "and we didn't have enough time to truly be each other's buddies in life, share something that others can't live without, a relationship…I don't want the feelings of anger, of wasted time, and a nonconnection we have the few times we are together when I am home. I don't know what I am saying or where this is leading to or how to really say what I want to say….I don't know how but I would like/love a relationship with you."

Matt told his father that he felt fragile and that his time in the military had damaged his ability to connect with other men. Nevertheless, he wanted to bury any past disagreements with his father and find a middle ground where they could connect. "I do often dream about a relationship with you some day; once we figure out the solution, my dreams will be a reality. I do love you and miss you dearly."

That email opened the communication gate between the two men. They still had a long way to go and Mike was determined to find a way to reconnect with his son.

Neither was aware they only had a handful of years left to forge that bond and become the friends that Matt had always wanted them to be.

The DeRemers visited Matt annually in California. Mike didn't always get to go, but after his son's email he went with Julie and Lynsey to visit Matt that June. The two of them finally had a face-to-face conversation about what living with bipolar disease was like for Matt. "Let me describe it to you," Matt told his father. "Having bipolar means I could completely destroy your house and after I'm done, not even remember I did it." He told his father about the depths of his mood swings, the inability to corral his mind, the whirring thoughts that consumed him.

"Matt," Mike said, "I don't care if you rob a bank. You're always going to be my son. I'm always going to love you."

That week, the family spent hours together, getting sushi, eating Mexican food, getting to know Crissy better, and gaining a peek inside Matt's world. Mike pulled Matt aside and asked his son what he wanted to do, some activity that could be just Dad and him.

"Go skydiving," was Matt's answer. He'd been doing it for months at this place in Lodi, and wanted to share the experience with his father. For Matt, skydiving helped clear his head, and ease the constant stress in his chest.

Mike was hesitant. Jumping out of an airplane at almost thirteen thousand feet? Then he saw how excited his son was and he couldn't say no. They arrived at the skydiving place and the minute Matt walked through the doors he was greeted like Norm in *Cheers*. Everyone knew him, everyone loved him.

Since it was his first jump, Mike went tandem, while Matt went solo. Mike's partner was, according to Matt, "The kind of guy who tells you what you need to know when you need to know it," which didn't exactly soothe Mike's nerves. Mike and his jump partner went first, sliding down a metal rail inside the plane to the open door, and then, before Mike could say no, out into the sky. They freefell for a little while, then the chute opened. Mike enjoyed a quiet, peaceful dive over the vineyards and Alcatraz, which the family had toured the day before.

As the ground grew ever closer, his partner coached him so he had perfect timing for an easy landing. Matt, who had hurried his dive so he could stand on the ground and watch his father come in, ran up to Mike as soon as his father touched down, proud and surprised at how easily his father had taken to skydiving.

It was a moment that deepened their bond and changed everything between Mike and Matt. "When he was little," Mike said, "I was always trying to get Matt to enjoy the things I did. Then I decided to do the things he liked to do and that's when we got really close."

Matt was always an expressive person, and the family often saved his holiday cards to read last because they would leave everyone in tears. One year, Matt sent a card just to his father, and although the card itself was marked by Matt's typical off-beat humor, the typed letter inside brought tears to Mike's eyes.

Dear Father,

When I look at the keys and try to put together what I want to say to you, I can only smile and get a little emotional. Although we have had our differences, we are working on our friendship and have really tried to hear each other out in what we are both doing in our individual lives. The biggest thing that I would like to express is how proud I am of you...You and I will always butt heads on our opinions, ideas and beliefs, because in the end, I am you. Whenever both of our lives are turned upside down because our relationship seems to be on the rocks, I remind myself that I have your mannerisms, your smile, your smooth swagger, the same speech pattern, your laugh, and I even tell jokes in a similar style...I am not only proud of you for fighting through life and accomplishing your goals through life higher than most fathom of having, but for changing your life...The change you made actually saved my life; my outlook on life has transitioned from a very dark place to a more humble approach. I look at people differently. I see things in a different light and I do strive to make things better than they were. This was only possible from your own transformation. You are my hero and I truly mean that with all my heart…I love you, Dad.

Your thankful son,
Matthew

If there was one thing evident in all of Matt's writings and in the family's stories, it is that the DeRemers love each other deeply. They speak of Matt often in the present tense, keeping their son with them as much today as before he passed away. Mike and Julie were given a son with a difficult mental illness, but they believe God did that for a reason—because they could love that boy through anything, and be there for him on the roller coaster that was his life. "We always came together as a family," Julie said. "We called ourselves the four Musketeers. Now it's the three Musketeers, but we're still living life and we're still coming together as a family."

Matt's death left an irrevocable hole in the DeRemers' world, but their support and strength during the years before his passing were part of what made Matt a man who left a deep imprint on everyone he met. People who became a part of his funeral, and later, became a part of carrying Matt's legacy forward into the world.

Chapter Nine

One of the ways Matt expressed himself was through the tattoos he inked on his body. He spent an inordinate amount of time planning, sketching, and discussing what he would engrave onto his body. Before he died, he had a total of thirteen tattoos on his chest, back, and arms. "I hate the pain," he wrote in his journal, "but the thought of having something put on me that describes who I am for all to see is what I'm all about. Keeps me occupied!"

By far, his most elaborate tattoo was the one that covered almost his entire back. He drew several sketches of what he wanted and dedicated pages and pages of his journals to his design ideas. Of this tattoo, he wrote, "This is a design capturing my creed to myself of who I am and why I joined the Marine Corps. It's also going to introduce within hidden places: Honor, Discipline, Courage, Commitment. The large prongs are Jr., Julio, Rickey, Dreamer. Tribal design. Equality is key. There must be balance within the design. In the center, it must seem as if it's a dark hole with a hellish outer rim, with my creed on one side and a mirror image on the other—exactly and equally."

Across the top of the tattoo, arching over the wings that spread from the center, he had written OVERCOME. Beneath that, the German words *Auberer Grenze*, which mean "outer limits." Before choosing *auberer grenze,* he listed several options for those two words: Life & Death, Fate & Destiny, Light & Dark, Happiness & Fear. In the end, outer limits most expressed how he felt about his life. "This sums up what I fight for," he wrote.

At the base of the tattoo, he had a dark bird with its wings spread. This he called his dark angel, the bipolar side of himself that he battled on a daily basis. The tattoo, with its warring images of light and dark, was evocative of how Matt viewed himself. "I look into myself and I see a split world. One side filled with beauty, peace throughout all. A place where hope fulfills all and only smiles are the currency needed for anything to be done. As you walk the edges of this realm, you can feel the flames of another. Hate and blood is the perfumed scent of this place. I see myself screaming [from] pain, games of confusion and selfishness to only worry about. I don't care if I live or die; the only pleasure I get is hurting myself as I put myself through hell. Dying within is what makes the flames [stay] lit."

"Every day seems to be a struggle because I chose a path where the direction is unsure. Second guessing myself is an every minute dilemma because I'm always pulled between right and wrong. Along with being alone, due to not knowing how to keep friends, my past is running through my mind as if it's an every-hour slideshow," he wrote while he was overseas in Iraq. "I have to put on a show while my uniform is on due to my commitment to an oath. I swore to keep the peace while being proper at all times. When in reality, I can't wait to take it all off and freefall, only feeling gravity pulling me down. A smile is on my face as I think of it now."

His family said that for much of Matt's life, his biggest battle was with himself—against his bipolar disease and against his depression. He wrote a lot of dark poetry over the years, all filled with themes of death and despair. All he wanted, they said, was to be loved as he was and to be at peace with himself.

When he returned to Florida in 2014, he rebuilt his relationship with God, and his tattoos and writing reflect that change in attitude. For weeks, he talked on Facebook about getting another tattoo. This one was simple, just the words: John 14:12, written in an elaborate script on his forearm.

That verse: "*Very truly I tell you, whoever believes in me will do the works I have been doing, and they will do even greater things than these, because I am going to the Father,*" became his motto for the latter part of his too-short life. He had found God and fully intended to hold on to that relationship, because that was where Matt DeRemer finally found some measure of peace. He would, however, have to ride through a few more difficult years...searching and failing for a way to live with his bipolar disorder and, most importantly, with himself.

Chapter Ten

A couple of years before he moved back to Florida, Matt found a job as a personal trainer at a gym in Pleasanton, CA, and thought he had found the perfect career. It didn't take long before he became disillusioned with that place, however, because he realized their bottom line was more about making money on memberships than on truly getting people healthy.

On top of that, his relationship with Crissy was struggling. He could see the impact his bipolar disorder was having on her and on himself. "I am awake to the fact that my intentions of staying with Crissy…just didn't last. True love has to be at the base before anything else. That was my intention at the start and into the middle; things did change over this past year, but too late, knowing that I will forever stay the way I am now without any change towards myself."

It would be another four months before Matt finally admitted the truth—he hadn't taken any medication since the previous fall. His hours were cut at work and then he was suspended for not handling membership signups according to corporate policy. He was suicidal at the end of 2011, which scared Crissy so much she called the suicide hotline and got him into a psychologist's office. That was the moment that got him back on track medically and shifted his behavior.

The meds made a difference. By February 2012, he had enrolled in college, he and Crissy were patching up their relationship, and his emails were less panicked and more optimistic. The roller coaster dipped down again by summer, however, and by June, Matt was "...slowly slipping into despair over the life I live."

His relationship with Crissy hit a seriously rough patch, and Matt began to "pray to God to show me truth in my actions and every time (in really weird ways), He showed me truths that I needed to see."

Matt continued to leave a destructive path in his wake throughout 2012. Things would smooth out, he'd settle into work and school, then he would go off his meds and his moods would drive away those who loved him—or he'd shut them out entirely.

However, as he neared the end of his twenties, he began to have more self realizations and apologized often for lashing out at his family. "I never wanted to be alone. I feel that pain now in my relationships and flings I have because I crave what I have always wanted...When I think about my past, I have to shake it off, remember not to blame because it truly doesn't matter now, and I have to fly by the seat of my pants from one choice to another because I really don't (and have never known) what I'm doing."

"...I am in a battle right now that no one can fix and no one needs to hear about because my head is my enemy. I can't talk to anyone because everyone chooses to see me as normal or read from some book they have read or secondhand advice, but never dealt with themselves. I know this now—there is no handbook for me and there is only firsthand knowledge to help me. If you haven't lived it, you can't speak it."

Matt was struggling to find a therapist in California who could understand and help him. The pain in his emails is evident, along with the acceptance of his disease as a permanent part of his makeup. "I'm f*^#ing tired of not fitting in, I'm tired of being tossed aside, and I am tired of being me. I love myself, I see my life as in terms of what I have are high quality, but what does that matter? In my head there is no heaven or hell anymore; my head is just full of everything."

As he had in high school when he would lay on her bed and talk for hours, Matt poured everything he felt onto the pages of his emails to his mom. He talked about wanting independence and distance, yet when his world got scary or stressful, he always returned to the family who loved him and knew him best. "I'm twenty-seven years old and f*^#ing scared," he wrote to his mother. "There hasn't been any treatment to battle this, my head has tricked everyone to leave it alone, and every day to step off the ledge because I am tired of seeing, hearing and doing what it wants."

As his relationship with Crissy deteriorated, so too did Matt. He dated another woman for a short time, a relationship that was toxic and volatile. It proved to be the last straw for Crissy, who refused one more attempt to reconcile after dozens of breakups and reunions. The skydiving that Matt loved so much had hurt his back and he had to quit, which devastated him. On top of that, the school he had enrolled in to get his surgical technology degree was losing its accreditation.

It was the middle of 2013 and Matt was at a crossroads. Between his time in the military and his time with Crissy, Matt spent eight years total in California, but now he realized the key to finding himself was back in Florida. He called his family, asking for help. Mike dropped everything, booked a flight, rented a Penske truck, and went to California to get his son.

Chapter Eleven

Mike and Matt drove straight through, fifty-one hours across the United States. They stopped for gas and food-to-go, with Matt opting for healthy options and Mike grabbing fast food. When Mike's ankles swelled from all the salt and sugar, Matt teased his father about his meal choices. Overall, it was a good trip, a chance for the two of them to talk and reknit the connection they had lost over the years.

Matt moved in with his family for a couple of weeks, while his mother helped get him enrolled at Southeastern College and find an apartment. He moved into a place located at the opposite end of the same street as his sister Lynsey's apartment. Matt relied on Lynsey to help him transition back into living alone and settling into school, which drew the now-adult siblings close together.

When Matt first returned to Florida, his heart and head were hurting. The music he chose to listen to echoed this pain—hardcore singers like Marilyn Manson with screaming lyrics and screeching guitars. "When I hear my hard-hitting, no feelings, unsocial, fast-paced thunder with screams in the background, I get in my zone," Matt wrote in his journal. "A place where no one can get in my personal space. These bands don't care what you think of them. They only make music, express themselves, the only way they know how to…loud, fast, and their feelings left on the table."

His mother, worried about her son and his sporadic medical compliance, took him to his appointments at the VA hospital. For years, Matt's emails and phone calls were her only barometers for her son's disease. Every other moment seemed to be a crisis with Matt and she thought maybe he was overexaggerating. She learned quickly that he wasn't. If anything, he had spared his family from some of the worst of his disorder.

The medication regime alone was intimidating. At one point, Matt had sixty-five bottles of pills in his cabinet. His angry outbursts would get destructive—he once pounded on Lynsey's car so hard, he broke her windshield. Another time, he was screaming at his mother while she drove, in a total meltdown about the errands he needed to run that day. Julie calmly told her son she was going to pull the car over, give him a piece of paper, and let him write down what he needed to accomplish.

Mike also saw the other side of his son's disease. When Mike was helping Matt sell his car, Matt descended into a full-blown panic attack in the parking lot, convinced that he had sold the car with his $700 helmet still inside. It took hours for Mike to calm Matt down after finally locating the helmet at the service shop.

As Matt stabilized on his medication, he learned to talk about what he was going through and his parents learned to recognize the signs of an impending mood swing. To help him stay consistent with his treatment, Julie organized his meds and tried talking him through the best options. Matt was overwhelmed. Between therapy, doctor appointments and going to school, he was frustrated that he was nearly thirty, unmarried and childless. He felt like he had lost a huge chunk of his life to bipolar disorder.

Then three things happened in his life at almost the same time—he got on the back of a motorcycle, he got close to God, and he met the woman who would eventually become his wife. These were milestones Matt reached in the eighteen months before he died, drawing him closer to the life he sought for almost three decades.

While he was in college, Matt was asked to take a motorcycle ride with Monique, a friend from class. After suffering with massive back pain, Matt had given up skydiving and was depressed at the thought he would never again be able to plummet through the sky like a bird. The motorcycle, however, gave him that feeling of flying, and after his first ride, he was hooked. He bought a 2014 Suzuki GSX-R750, and nicknamed her Sweet Pea. On the side of his bike, he engraved his favorite Bible verse, John 14:6, "*I am the way, the truth, the life. No man comes to God except through Me.*"

He had been actively trying to get to know God by reading his Bible and attending church, something he'd started doing back in California. He found a Christ-centered men's motorcycle club named Fastlane for Christ and joined them. There, he found people with a similar passion for speed and God.

He read often, diving into the Bible over and over again for answers and returning several times to a book by Joyce Meyers titled *Battlefield of the Mind: Winning the Battle of Your Mind.* The book talks about overcoming depression and negative thoughts by learning to turn one's thoughts to God instead of worry and fear, a topic that Matt found fascinating and helpful as he struggled to do that within himself. He was also a fan of John Eldredge's *Wild at Heart: Discovering the Secret of a Man's Soul.*

As with his bodybuilding, Matt took copious notes about his path with God. As he saw his life becoming more peaceful, he reached out more to Christ. He wrote down a prayer that he set in front of himself every morning, whispering these words before breakfast:

God,

I am thankful for:

- *Never letting me go and keeping me on my path even though I don't understand the turns. You have guided me.*
- *For looking out for my best interests*
- *For always providing me all the comforts that allow me to stay calm and true to who I am—shelter, transportation, skill, ambition*
- *Thank you for creating me perfect in Your image*
- *The family that always backs me on every aspect of life*
- *For the relationships that make me learn more about myself, what I really want. That You are in control of me. In ultimate control of my time. A*

lifelong relationship with the one You will ultimately choose to be in my life "till death do us part"

- *For the career I have chosen and the future it will provide*
- *For all the people who got me through*
- *For always being on my side and guiding me*
- *For a path, for a purpose for me to serve*
- *I have faith, I have trust in You and You are my Holy Father.*

On the flip side, he kept a list of things he wanted God to forgive him for doing. Things familiar to so many of us—his need to control the outcome of events, his cursing, the way that he sometimes turned away from God when he was in a relationship, for being hypocritical, and for living in the flesh instead of spiritually.

And in a theme that was so evocative of Matt's struggle to love himself, he wrote asking for God's grace, "...for failing You, Your love, and always asking for mercy, only to move onto another addiction to keep me satisfied for the moment and not facing You and myself."

When Matt went to his parents, depressed that he hadn't yet achieved all he wanted to, his mother reminded him that failure was a part of life. The DeRemer kids were allowed to try any sport or activity they wanted, to spread their wings and find what they enjoyed. Like anyone, they weren't always successful, but those setbacks brought just as many lessons as the successes. "When you are failing, you are learning, Matt," Julie assured him.

Matt replied with the line he had used dozens of times over the years when things got hard or the family was struggling. "You're right, Mom. We're dreamers. We'll figure it out."

And they did—all through the next year, not knowing it would be the last with all of them together.

Chapter Twelve

In 2014, Matt found BridgePoint Church. The St. Petersburg church was growing and had an active, enthusiastic congregation, and warm and welcoming leadership. Matt loved the church and ended up inviting his parents to join him. "Happy happy happy Sunday!" he wrote on Facebook in September. "It's always good to lose things in life that you rely on, depend on, and cherish more than God....Why? Because through EXTREME pain comes EXTREME GROWTH, doors will open that haven't ever been open before and finally (or once again) your eyes are open to God and all His glory. I have said it many many many times, once you get a taste of God's happiness from heaven there is no turning back! Every day I live by 3 things and strive by them: Faith, hope, and (above all) love. Anyone need to talk about anything? Please feel free to hit me up, I'm here to listen!"

His life was finally on an upswing. Earlier that year, he had graduated from college and found a part-time job at WestBay Surgical Center. In April, he met a woman named Denise on Facebook. The two hit it off immediately and agreed to meet halfway between their homes for a first date. Matt was head over heels in an instant, and soon his days revolved around work, church, his bike, and Denise.

He reconnected with Rick and Julio, as well as his old high school friend, Brett, who had the same passion for bodybuilding. Through Brett, Matt met a trainer named Nick, who helped him get his diet and workouts back on track. Everything was aligning and Matt was overjoyed.

Matt thought he had found the perfect match in Denise and proposed after only a couple of months. She said yes and they made it official that July, in a quick courthouse ceremony with just their families in attendance. They barely knew each other, and coupled with Matt's bipolar disorder, the marriage was too much, too fast.

Matt had high hopes, but within weeks Denise had moved out and Matt was left alone once again. His mother came over and found her son sobbing, unsure of what to do or how to save his marriage. "Now I see that how I act and treat people only brings me loneliness, and no peace of mind!" he wrote that year.

Matt opted to try marriage counseling at BridgePoint Church. He thought if he brought everything back to God, then maybe their relationship could be saved. He was determined to get his bipolar disorder under control and to live in a more selfless way. "He was so easy to love," Julie said, "but so hard to live with."

Still, he kept going to counseling, determined to find the key to a happy wife and a happy life. He realized that their jobs were a huge part of the problem. They worked opposite hours, which left him alone too much, and triggered his bipolar disorder. "Sunday is an explosion [day] because I'm mad about Monday through Friday."

He wrote long notes about what he saw as his role in the demise of his relationships. "I have been passive, giving all of me, my money, my resources, my blinding love, only to be left when I become too attached and affectionate. I get angry and lose control due to not receiving the love given like at the beginning of meeting them." When the women he loved walked away from him, he felt "pain, unquestionable amounts of pain."

He found several translations of Ephesians 5:33, which says, "However, each one of you also must love his wife as he loves himself, and the wife must respect her husband." To Matt, this meant that a husband should obey the command to love and respect his wife, even if his wife is not doing the same, and vice versa. At the bottom of that page, he wrote four simple words: *Faith gets you through.*

His wife didn't understand his bipolar disorder, which left Matt feeling even more isolated. His struggle to explain it to her was no more successful than his efforts with his other girlfriends or family. The whirling dervish that could be Matt's mind was almost incomprehensible to those who didn't know him deeply.

Despite all of that, Matt's optimism and joy for his new life in Florida was evident in his Facebook posts. He had found God, and through that discovered peace and happiness. "The last three services for the last three Sundays has been the same message over and over and over again," he wrote on September 20th. "After explaining what a person looks like when they live in the world vs. living with and for God, the question that was asked at the end of the service was: When are you going to start? Are you looking for something to fill a hole that has never been filled before? Are you looking for an endless lifelong cause, and/or are you looking for a feeling that's never been felt? And/or are you a Christian that has never served God only for yourself (meaning living a selfless life, not about you, but all and only for God's will)? If you're ready for your life to really change, start today."

Matt would post inspirational memes and messages to the hundreds of friends he had made all over the world. That same month, he had posted an image of two words: *Be Patient.*

"Sometimes you have to go through the worst to get to the best," he wrote beside the image. "Testimonies are meant to move you, help guide decisions you have to make in your life, and to wipe away cobwebs. Throughout my own journey, I have been praying to God, 'I want to serve others, I want to reach one person at a time, and I want to share the word'...To everyone and anywhere and anytime...today was a major first step towards that idea of my future...humbled, honored, and taking a step back to take it all in."

He was finding himself and finding his place in the world. For a man who had lived across the country and across the world, struggling to fit in his entire life, Matt was finally feeling at home. "Waking up to another day to prove that through the dark, it's possible to shine bright," he wrote in October. "I'm blessed to not have a one-track mind and living through emotions and feelings, well, even though it's always a rollercoaster, I wouldn't change it one bit. I know no one like me and that, that is always something to cherish."

Almost every day in those last few months of his life, he expressed gratitude for his journey, his friends, and his family. "I have been truly blessed to live a life with no regrets, many wake-up calls, and to view life at its most extremes."

He had no idea that he had less than three months left on earth, or that the simple messages he posted would go on to change hundreds of people's lives.

Chapter Thirteen

Do Not Fear Death. Fear a Life of Mediocrity.

Several times, Matt posted messages on his Facebook page with that saying. That was Matt to a T—he lived a life that was far beyond mediocre and, even though he died at thirty-one, he experienced things few people get to do in three times as many years of life. He traveled, he served his country, he found his passion, and he jumped out of planes and sped down highways. He loved and he lost, and throughout it all he gave back to the people who loved him.

Family was the most important thing in Matt's life. He loved his family, fought with his family, made up with them again. But most of all, he respected and admired them. He wrote dozens of emails to his parents and sister, telling them how proud he was of their accomplishments. A few months after he returned to Florida, he wrote a letter to his mother and in it, called her 'a warrior'.

He talked about how she had inspired him, and rescued him over and over again. "You are by far the most inspirational person I know. It took me many years to see your unconditional love."

The one-page letter went on to say how Matt admired that Julie stood up to the naysayers and fought for their family in every way. "When you talk, people should listen, when you teach, people should take notes, and wherever you walk, people should follow."

Yet, he still struggled with forgiving himself. He knew what his bipolar disorder had put his family through, and Matt's regrets ran deep. He spoke in his journals about wanting a do-over, a chance to make it all right with the people who had been by his side. "Once again," he told his mother, "I am still putting you through a struggle that makes me pray every night how to stop all this to get back to my feet. I wish I could give you more."

By the end of his life, Matt's relationship with his father had come full circle. They had shared skydiving, and in those last few months the two of them shared a common love of bikes. On September 20th, they took their motorcycles out for a ride together. His Facebook post was a simple couple of lines: "Today: what a proud day it is. First time riding with my dad."

Three months exactly, on December 20, 2015, he took his last ride with his father. Matt was proud as punch of being with his dad and thrilled to share his passion with the man he so admired. They rode through Tampa, stopped by Maggiano's for lunch, and returned home, a winding, easy pace that gave them hours together to just enjoy the sunshine and each other's company. "I'm blessed, why?" Matt wrote on Facebook. "Because my dad is my hero. Great ride, laughed 99% of the time (unless we were racing), and always has great stories to tell on any occasion!"

Matt worked hard to find that connection with God by reading, journaling, and going to church. He surrounded himself with like-minded people so he could be inspired by their lessons and advice. He also changed his lifestyle to reflect his connection with God. Gone was the Marilyn Manson type shock rock, replaced by Christian music and a quieter, gentler atmosphere in his apartment. "To be healed from pain," he posted on November 1st, "doesn't mean lifting the [veil] from it but to live through the struggle in joy knowing that God has you. Again, I am more grateful now for what is than what used to be."

Still, he struggled to accept himself, to see himself as the perfect being God created. "God, Holy Father, Jesus, my faith is in this, my life, my alteration is in Your hands. Clean me from all the years of sin I have covered myself in and turn me back into the perfection you once made me," he wrote.

That year, he had chosen to read *Jesus Calling*, a devotional by Sarah Young. He copied the message from December 4th onto his Facebook page. The passage talks about the importance of listening to God's voice, something Matt admitted he had trouble doing, because if there was one thing Matt rarely was, it was quiet. "I don't do well with meditation, downtime, and ways to approach my own time off; now I see through my transition that everything is the way it should be."

"You are a man of noise," his mother often told him. "God talks to you in the quiet times, Matt. His Word is there. You just have to listen."

Through the month of December 2015, Matt must have been listening because he told his mother in a text on December 9th that he wasn't 'long for this world'. Panicked, Julie asked him if he was feeling suicidal and he assured her that he had no plans to take his own life, but that he could feel his days slipping away. "My time is very near," he wrote. "And I want to get things in order."

He had lunch with his mother a few days later, and on the paper tablecloth Matt wrote down his list of goals for the coming year. He wanted to find a cheaper place to live, one that was closer to work and his parents. He wanted to pay down his debts and he wanted to give up most of his material goods. He told Julie that since he had found and accepted Christ, "I have become selfless. I'm no longer selfish."

That very day, he asked his mother to go to the bank with him to help him pay off a debt to a friend. It had to be that day, Matt insisted. He didn't want to delay a single second on any of his plans.

God seemed to have His hand in all the little moments of that last month. The day before Matt died, he was pulled over for having expired tags on his motorcycle. His mother had earlier paid the re-registration fees as a surprise for his birthday, so she and Matt went down to the tax collector's office that day to clear up the confusion. While there, he insisted on having his mother listed as the next of kin on his license. Should something happen to him, he said, he wanted his parents to know right away.

Perhaps God had been telling Matt something that he hadn't shared with those around him. In an almost heartbreaking and prophetic moment, Matt had written in his journal at the beginning of 2015 that he was on "a one-year journey to find myself in God's image."

Above and beyond that, Matt wanted to share with other people how finding the love of Christ had changed his life in fundamental ways. On one difficult night, he sat down with his father and asked Mike how he could get closer to God. Mike took a piece of paper and drew a vertical line on either side, then put a valley in between the two lines. He labeled the first line MATT and the second line GOD. "This is you and God," he told his son. "There's a gap between the two of you. What fills that space and what keeps you from getting to God is sin. But this," he drew a cross between the lines, "is how you get to God. Jesus Christ is the bridge between you. You just have to trust in that and in God's plan. It's as simple as that, Matt."

After his death, a fellow rider from the motorcycle club came up to his parents at the funeral. "I wish I had saved the cocktail napkin Matt gave me," she said. "On it, he had drawn this diagram about how to accept Christ in your life."

Matt, so excited about his relationship with Christ, had taken his father's lesson and brought it to everyone he could. He didn't care if he was in a bar or at someone's home. On napkins and in his words, Matt spread that message about crossing the divide between us and God to the people in his life. As his father had promised him, finding the way was as simple as that.

By the end of his life, Matt had accepted his bipolar disorder as part of God's plan, and finally discovered love for himself...a love that allowed him to give those around him a deep, true, and everlasting connection in return. In the space of that one year, he wrote, he wanted to find "love in all people—see the world as God sees it."

Those handwritten words are on a paper entitled "Personal Things I Pray For," one of several sheets in a folder Matt named *My Path With God.* When he returned to Florida, Matt took hold of God's hand and followed the path He set before him. In leaving this world, he allowed those who knew him to pick up the end of his journey and embark on their own. Finding love in all people, a lesson taught by a man who spent three decades searching for that very thing.

Chapter Fourteen

The meaning of life is to find your gift. The purpose of life is to give it away.

Matt wrote that on his Facebook wall about a month before he died. He probably had no idea that his gift would be a few simple words, a single social media post that lit up the world and made people everywhere stop, think, and count their blessings.

More than eight hundred people attended Matthew Gordon DeRemer's funeral. The biker community showed up in force, with dozens of bikers hanging their leather cuts from the balcony of the church, alongside a parachute from his skydiving friends. Matt was given a full military funeral, with a motorcycle procession from the church to the cemetery. The ride traversed the Tampa Skyway Bridge, a route Matt himself had taken hundreds of times. When Mike rode across the bridge, he carried several treasured things of his son's. As he crossed that bridge, two of Matt's bandanas were caught in the wind, whisked away and up, until they were too far away to be seen.

The DeRemers have mementos of Matt all around their house. Pictures of their son's infectious grin, the flag that draped his casket, the poems and letters he wrote to them. His favorite books sit on the table beside the armchair in the living room. His motorcycle helmet and bow and arrows sit on shelves, waiting for a man who will never return. Matt's radio sits in Mike's office, and when Mike went to turn it on one day, the radio was still tuned to Joy FM, the local Christian station that brought Matt so much peace in the last year of his life. "To this day," Mike said, "I don't know how he did all that he did, with his mind going like it did. I would have given up."

Julie misses the days when Matt would lie on her bed and talk for hours. They would debate big decisions Matt had to make, or talk about cases he had dealt with, in the common language of people working in the same field. "He was so intelligent. I miss his voice. I miss the noise."

Lynsey talks of her brother with pride and admiration for how much living he did in such a short time. "His life showed that he lived above his bipolar disease. He lived beyond that diagnosis."

The DeRemers are heartbroken, and will forever mourn the son they loved so dearly. Matt had a larger than life personality, a smile that drew everyone close, and love for every person he met, regardless of race, gender, or orientation. He was one of the most accepting people anyone knew, maybe because he knew what it was like to be an outsider.

A few weeks after his death, the employees at Bellair Surgical Center (where Matt had started working a few months earlier) called and asked if they could "meet the people Matt talked about every day." When they got there, they were introduced to the man who had been hired to take Matt's position. "I can't ever fill his shoes," the young man told Matt's family. "He was one of a kind."

Everywhere they go, the DeRemers meet someone who was touched by Matt, either in person or by Matt's words that went viral. "I loved him; I loved talking to him," one nurse told Mike when he went in for cataract surgery. "He loved people. He was infectious to be around." The family often receives emails and social media posts from total strangers who were moved by Matt's prophetic words.

"I don't really know where I'll end up tonight, but I do know where I wind up is where I am meant to be."

Where he was meant to be is where he will remain forever—in the hearts of hundreds of people who were honored to know a man who refused to be hobbled by a diagnosis, who lived his life out loud, and who saw love as a risk worth taking. That was Matthew DeRemer's gift to the world, as unique and impossible to contain as the man himself. He *was* a light—beautiful, bright, warm and absolutely unforgettable.

A Word from the Family

From Matt's Parents

Most people will agree that their family is dysfunctional. My wife and I grew up in environments like that, maybe because of the lack of love and acceptance we were given in our childhood homes. Early on, Julie and I were determined to show our love to both of our children, Lynsey and Matthew. Because of that, our family unit has always been number one. It is through this connection that we have faced the loss of Matthew. They say blood is thicker than water, and in our case, it is true.

We used to be a strand of four; now we are a strand of three. Strands tied together are stronger than one single strand. Our hope and prayer is that through reading the story of our son, all of you will become stronger as a family.

Matt tattooed his left forearm with the Bible verse found in the Gospel of John, John 14:12. It is this verse that has driven our family to scour all of Matt's journals, poems, personal letters, and pictures to let the world know that there is hope—hope for battles with illness, hope for struggles in families, and hope for finding God and peace. We believe that this book will change lives and allow people to heal, both physically and spiritually.

God promises in the Bible to give His creation an abundant life, showering us with blessing after blessing. Our family has been truly blessed to have had Matthew as our son; brother to Lynsey. His life was a bright, brilliant, shooting star.

We are proud of the young man he became. In just a short span, he has touched and changed many lives, and we pray that through his story, his legacy will continue. This is only the beginning, for as John 14:12 states, "... and he will do even greater things because I (Jesus) am going to the Father."

Mike DeRemer
Julie DeRemer

From Matt's Sister

I can remember both hard and joyful times with my brother. We were allowed to be individuals and were encouraged by our parents to look beyond what was in front of us. I can honestly say that I never considered the masks of bravado and charisma that Matt wore as a disguise for his pain until we were both older.

He ran towards others and sought genuine friends wherever he was. There was a magnetic pull to him. Matt always encouraged me to come out of my own shell and live life out loud. There were so many joyful times with him and our family.

During the painful times of his life, Matt's reactions confused me. I wanted to help but knew that I was not equipped to fix the pain. My prayers for him were constant. Although Matt was physically stronger, I always wanted to protect him, as an older sister should.

It was not hard to love Matt, but not having a complete understanding of what he was going through was difficult. We did fight, but it was not a rivalry in my mind. With time, we both had experiences that opened our perspectives and showed us areas of compromise with each other.

When Matt moved back to Florida, we both attended the same college. I went to night school for medical assisting and he attended in the day for surgical tech. I can still remember buying snacks for a fundraiser for his program. Both the teacher and students were surprised when I told them who my brother was. We graduated in the same ceremony. Even in my wildest imagination, I would not have thought that Matt and I would be starting new careers in the same industry together.

My parents and brother had been going to BridgePoint Church, and I naturally followed. We had not attended the same church as a family in years. At BridgePoint, we found a place for all of us. Our family bond was strong before this but after we found a church together, it grew to titanium strength.

In the last year of his life, Matt became the man of God that he was meant to be. My prayers for him never ceased. The details of his journey were kept by God, but the inspiration of his faithful growth was felt and put into action.

On the night of December 31st, 2015, we all felt a nagging sense of foreboding. Matt never changed his plans without telling us. After Mom and Dad talked to the state trooper, I got a call from Mom saying that they were on the way over. My heart already knew that the news would not be good.

The next day I went to his apartment and while I was there, I received a message from a friend with a link to the first newspaper article about the crash. Sensing the coming social media storm, I posted a simple, honoring message about my brother, to let people know about Matt's death. The immediate outpouring of love for our family was amazing. Matt's legacy was one of God's pure joy and love.

We are almost at two years now since he died and life has moved on. We are still meeting people that knew Matt and were inspired by his presence in their lives. As his sister, I am touched by these encounters, but I am still working on finding my voice in all that has happened. I will never know another person like Matt.

Lynsey DeRemer

Afterword and Resources

In writing this book, I grew to know a man I had never met. As an author, I felt an enormous weight of responsibility to do justice to Matt's story, to depict him accurately and fairly, and to do so with the same love that those who knew him felt. His family had kept all of his journals and in reading them, I found a man who was complex and inspiring. Matt struggled with so many things in life, but no matter how much darkness entered his mind, he returned to one fundamental over and over:

Love.

Matt loved his family. Loved his friends. Loved the women in his life. And in the end, he loved the Lord more than he ever thought possible. I wish I could have included all of his wonderful letters, poems, and entries, because there was so much heart and soul in his handwritten words.

When Skip Watkins first brought us Matt's story, we were all moved beyond words at what had happened to him. Skip's research helped me understand Matt better, which made the writing easier.

I don't get emotional easily, but I did with this book. When I typed the line from Matt's journal about being on a one-year quest to get to know God (a heartbreaking entry because Matt didn't know that would be the final year he would be given), I cried. When I realized Matt had been reading the same devotional in his last year that I am reading the year I wrote this, I cried. I had to take some time before I started Chapter Fourteen, because even though I knew how the story ended, I didn't want to write those last few pages because I didn't want to let go of Matt. The last words in this book blurred through my tears. In writing his story, and getting to know his incredible family, I loved Matt, too.

My hope is that you can see him as I have—complicated and loving and extraordinary. No person is one-dimensional, but Matt DeRemer seemed to have an extra dimension that made him special and unforgettable. It was an incredible honor to write his story, and I pray it moves you as much as it moved me.

Shirley Jump

MOT
YCLI

Resources

This is by no means a complete list, but hopefully it provides more information on bipolar disorder, PTSD, and mental health.

National Suicide Prevention Hotline (US)
Phone: (800) 273-TALK (8255)

National Alliance for the Mentally Ill (NAMI)
3803 N. Fairfax Drive, Suite 100
Arlington, VA 22203
Phone: (703) 524-7600 or (800) 950-NAMI (Helpline)

www.Nami.org

Depression and Bipolar Alliance
55 E. Jackson Blvd, Suite 490
Chicago, Illinois 60604
Toll-free: (800) 826-3632
Fax: (312) 642-7243

www.dbsalliance.org/

Massachusetts General Hospital Neurology Forums
https://neurosurgery.mgh.harvard.edu/WebForum.htm

PTSD: National Center for PTSD Home
U.S. Department of Veterans Affairs
810 Vermont Avenue
NW Washington DC 20420

Veterans Crisis Line:
1-800-273-8255 (Press 1)

www.ptsd.va.gov

This book is dedicated to
Matthew "Dreamer" DeRemer

December 26, 1984 to December 31, 2015

John 14:12, "Very truly I tell you, whoever believes in me will do the works I have been doing, and they will do even greater things than these, because I am going to the Father."